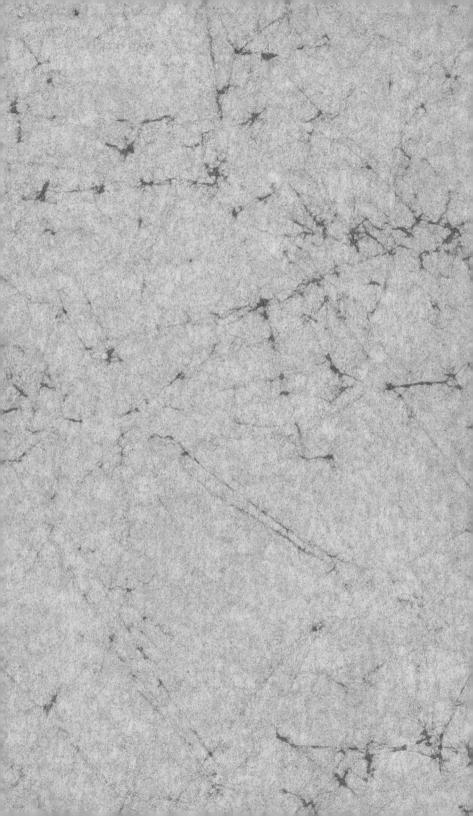

Eyewitness Accounts of the American Revolution

Narrative of the Fleet Under Lord Howe

Thomas L. O'Beirne

The New York Times & Arno Press

A

CANDID AND IMPARTIAL

N A R R A T I V E

OF THE

T R A N S A C T I O N S

OF THE

F L E E T,

UNDER THE COMMAND OF

L O R D H O W E,

FROM THE ARRIVAL OF THE TOULON SQUADRON, ON
THE COAST OF AMERICA, TO THE TIME OF HIS
LORDSHIP'S DEPARTURE FOR ENGLAND.

WITH

O B S E R V A T I O N S.

BY AN OFFICER THEN SERVING IN THE FLEET.

THE SECOND EDITION, REVISED AND CORRECTED,

WITH A PLAN OF THE SITUATION OF THE FLEET,
WITHIN SANDY-HOOK.

L O N D O N:
PRINTED FOR J. ALMON, OPPOSITE BURLINGTON-
HOUSE, PICCADILLY.

Explanation of the Plate.

THE anchors laid out on the larboard fide of the fhips in the line, were defigned as fprings to heave their broadfides up, to oppofe any force that might attempt to come up the channel.

The Vigilant, Phenix and Prefton were advanced to command the bar, to annoy the French fleet in paffing it, and to endeavour to throw them into confufion, after which they were to drop into the rear of the fleet.

The four galleys were ranged acrofs the narrow part of the channel, abreaft the Hook; from which fituation, in cafe of an attack, they could row in upon the fhoal, and cannonade at fuch diftance as fhould be moft convenient for the purpofe of annoying the enemy; their fituation on the fhoal would effectually prevent their being cut off.

The St. Albans and frigates were defigned for a moving and occafional force, and lay within the line.

The figures mark the depth at low water.

ADVER-

ADVERTISEMENT.

THE defign of the following Narrative, is to do juftice to a great and good man, by the beft mode of juftification that can be offered in his favour; a plain ftate of facts, an impartial account of his actions, fubmitted to public view. The writer acknowledges that he has not the honour of being in Lord Howe's fecrets, or of being even diftantly connected with him: yet the facts he relates will bear the ftricteft fcrutiny, in point of truth; and his obfervations on thofe facts, fhall be fuch as he formed on the fpot; as arofe from his own feelings at the time, or were fuggefted to him by officers of the firft character, both in the navy and army. If he affign the reafons and motives of any of his Lordfhip's operations, or advert to the inftructions and intelligence communicated to him from home, he does it from fubfequent information, and chiefly from his Lordfhip's public letters.

He fhall endeavour as much as poffible to avoid a technical ftyle; for he wifhes to be underftood

derftood by every clafs of readers, at the fame
time he does think it neceffary to apologize to
the public for obtruding on them the rough un-
polifhed language of a feaman, little verfed in
the elegancies of compofition, and unambitious
of the praife of a brilliant diction, or the fmooth
flow of well-rounded periods. He fhall often
have occafion to advert to our prefent difgraceful
fituation; and fome times to look forward to
thofe additional miferies which infallibly await
our perfeverance in the deftructive meafures
hitherto purfued, by a weak, ignorant Miniftry:
and while he points out to his oppreffed country-
men the deftroying fword, hanging over their
heads, and fufpended but by a fingle hair, he
cannot think that any among them will be fo
egregioufly trifling, as to fpend the time in exa-
mining its point, or determining whether it glit-
ters or not.

His chief apology fhould be to the noble Lord,
whofe actions he attempts to relate. It will
prove no very acceptable fervice, he fears, to his
lordfhip, to be brought thus forward; or that a
ftranger fhould attempt what his own connec-
tions feem, by their filence, to think unneceffary.
But he owns he has not philofophy enough to
ftifle his indignation, when he fees his gallant
Commander, whom he has learned to revere for

every

every great and good quality that can adorn the man or the officer, at the mercy of a fet of men, whofe intereft it is to undermine his character, and mifreprefent his conduct. He thinks the public have a right to be informed of the important fervices Lord Howe has rendered to his country; and of the ungrateful return he has met with at the hands, not of his country, but of fome of the fervants of the crown.

The narrative is confined to that period, in which the writer had the honour to ferve under his lordfhip. His conduct in America, previous to that time, when thoroughly inveftigated, will prove to have been of a piece with the whole tenot of his life; will redown to his own houour, and the difappointment and confufion of his enemies.

A CAN-

A

CANDID AND IMPARTIAL

NARRATIVE.

IN confequence of the advices from England, with which the Porcupine arrived in the Delaware, in the beginning of May, Lord Howe began immediately to collect his fcattered force. To the furprize of thofe who were ignorant of his motives, he called in his cruizers from the Chefapeak, and the other parts of the coaft, and ordered the large fhips from Rhode Ifland and New York to affemble at the mouth of the Delaware. The tranfports and victuallers were cleared from the wharves of Philadelphia with as much expedition as the moving of the army would admit; and on the 18th of June, Sir H. Clinton having completed the evacuation of Philadelphia, and entered the Jerfeys on his rout to

New

New York, the whole fleet affembled below Reedy Ifland. The large fhips, as well thofe which had been ordered from Newport, as thofe which were ftationed in the harbour of New York, were very imprudently detained by Rear Admiral Gambier, from the idea of the Vice Admiral being on the point of failing for that port.

On leaving the Delaware, which calms and contrary winds rendered impracticable till the 28th of June, Lord Howe divided the fleet into different fquadrons, each fquadron under the immediate infpection of particular Captains, and ordering Captain Hammond to remain about the Capes, with fome light cruizers, proceeded in the Eagle to New York, attended by the Trident, carrying the Commiffioners, and the Maidftone frigate.

The fleet was particularly fortunate in its paffage. The Eagle anchored at the Hook, the day [*June* 29.] after fhe had cleared Cape Henlopen, and we all joined her the following evening. By equal good fortune, Sir H. Clinton gained the Heights of Neverfink the fucceeding morning, after a long and fatiguing march. Wafhington had, for feveral days, hung on his rear, and harraffed him by fmall parties, till by endeavouring, on the 28th, to cut off the baggage of the Englifh army, he brought on a fharp

action

action at Freehold, wherein our rear guard repulsed two large detachments under La Fayette and Lee, and beat them back to the main body of the rebel army, pursuing them for four miles with much slaughter. The chief loss sustained by the Britith, was the death of Col. Monkton, one of the bravest officers in the army, and of the best beloved.

June 29. The morning of the day on which Lord Howe arrived at the Hook, he was met at sea by the Grantham packet, express from England. She brought advice that the Toulon squadron had sailed for America on the 15th of April; and informed his Lordship, that she had been been chased by them, in a southern latitude, at no great distance from the coast. Her dispatches, bearing date the 2d of May, mentioned a strong reinforcement to be sent immediately under Vice Admiral Byron *for Halifax.*

The utmost expedition was now requisite to take off the troops, that, with the transports and victuallers, they might be placed in safety, and the fleet got in readiness for sea, to act as circumstances should require, and with a view to the destination of the squadron under Admiral Byron. The enemy did not dare to pass the heights of Middleton. The sick and wounded were therefore embarked without molestation, and the artillery and baggage taken off, while a bridge of

B

boats

boats was throwing over the channel that fepa-
rates Sandy-Hook from the main. This work
was intrufted to Captain Duncan, and executed
with the ufual zeal and promptitude of that vigilant and induftrious officer. On the 5th of
July the whole army paffed into the ifland, and
from thence were carried in flat boats on board the
fleet, without the lofs of a man. Lord Howe
attended in perfon, as ufual ; and by his prefence
animated the zeal, and quickened the induftry,
of officers and men.

This important fervice was fcarce performed,
and Commodore Hotham, with the men of war
that lay off the town of New-York, arrived at
the Hook, [*July* 7.] when a lieutenant from
Captain Gardiner, whom the vice Admiral had
difpatched to the fouthward on the firft of *July*,
returned in a letter of marque, acquainting his
Lordfhip, that the Toulon fquadron was feen
by the Maidftone, on the coaft of Virginia, the
5th of the month. That, by their courfe, they
feemed at firft to be bound for the Chefapeak ;
but that on attending their motions to the morning of the 8th, Captain Gardiner had left them
at anchor in the Delaware. This account was
confirmed the fame evening, by the arrival of the
Roebuck, and fome of our fmall cruizers ; and
while the vice-admiral was employed, in confequence, in collecting his fmall force, and preparing

4

every

for every emergency, the captain of the Zebra arrived [*July* 11.] on board the Eagle, bringing
intelligence, that a fleet of 12 sail two-decked
ships, and three frigates, appeared the evening before, under French colours, holding their course
for New-York. At 12 o'clock the same day,
a signal was made, from one of our frigates without the bar, that they had hove in sight ; and in
the afternoon they were observed to come to anchor off Shrewsbury inlet, about four miles from
Sandy-Hook.

It is not in the power of words to do justice to
the spirit that blazed forth throughout the navy
and army on this occasion. Six sail of fixty-four
gun ships, three of fifty, two of forty, with some
frigates and sloops, for the most part wretchedly
manned, were all the force Lord Howe had to op-
pose to twelve sail of two-deck ships, and three
frigates. Of these one carried 90 guns, one 80,
six were of 74 guns, three of 64, one of 50 ;
the least of the frigates mounted 36. Their
complement in men was above eleven thousand.
Yet the spirit of Britons, roused by the superior
genius of one man, and influenced to second his
exertions to a height of emulation scarcely paral-
leled in history, set them at defiance.

A thousand volunteers from the transports pre-
sented themselves to man the fleet. Scarce could
the agents detain sufficient hands for the watch of

their

their refpective fhips. Many, whofe names were omitted in the lifts given in to the adjutant of the fleet, were found concealed in the boats which carried their more fortunate companions on board the feveral men of war. The army, idolatrous of the admiral's character, were equally forward and impatient to fignalize their zeal, in a line of fervice, new, and, independent of the fpirit that animated them, unpleafant and difgufting to men unaccuftomed to a fea-life. The grenadiers and light-infantry fcarcely recruited from the fatigues of a toilfome and dangerous march ; many of the officers with their wounds ftill green, were obliged to caft lots, to determine the companies which, with the general's approbation, were accepted to ferve as marines---The mafters and mates of the merchantmen and traders in the harbour, folicited employment with equal earneftnefs and fpirit. Several of them took their ftations at the guns with the common failors : others obtained permiffion to put out to fea in their fmall fwift-failing fhallops, to alarm fuch fhips as might be bound for the port, and to look out for Byron's fleet, if fortunately it fhould reach the coaft. One, in particular, his name was Duncan, with a fpirit of difinterefted bravery, and in language worthy of an old Roman, wrote for leave to convert his fhip, the whole hopes of his fortune, into a fire-veffel, to be conducted

ducted by himself; rejecting every mention of reward.

In this struggle of magnanimity, it was observed, with rapture, that the spirit which had raised the British nation above the rest of Europe for so many ages past, was not extinct; that it only wanted to be awakened, and properly directed, to blaze out with as bright a lustre as ever distinguished the most fortunate and brilliant of our days. From the commanders and officers those sallies of heroism were naturally expected ; their education, the seeds planted in their minds from their earliest infancy, and cherished by the spirit of their profession, it was natural to expect would produce such sentiments as fit and prepare the mind for these sudden and trying emergencies. But in the common men it was the spontaneous growth of the soil we saw exuberantly breaking forth ; and as long as this flourished, there could be no reason to despair of the health and vigour of the country.

Such were the sentiments, such the reflections throughout the fleet and army ; and all gloried in them, as reflecting honour on their country. But what must have been the feelings of that man, who shared the glory with his country ; and who, notwithstanding the unaffected modesty of his character, must have been conscious that all this zeal and emulation, in both corps,

was

was as much perfonal to himfelf, as he boafted it to be national?

Encouraged by fuch earnefts of determined bravery in the men, and affured of the merit and fkill of his feconds and officers, he loft not a moment in forming his difpofition. The Eagle and Trident, the Ifis, Roebuck, Phœnix, and Pearl, which had moved up to Staten Ifland to take in water, with the Ardent, from which Gambier had been ordered to fhift his flag, fell down from the watering place on the firft intimation of the approach of the French. A contrary wind preventing them from joining the detachment of the fquadron that had been left at the Hook, with all the expedition the danger feemed to require, the vice admiral quitted the Eagle, and throwing himfelf into his barge, haftened to the fhips below. But D'Eftaing, inftead of croffing the bar immediately, in the hope of furprifing our fleet, which it was natural to fuppofe he came prepared to attempt ., anchored, as is mentioned before, at the diftance of four miles from the Hook.

Here he remained for feveral days, employed at times in founding the bar, and wearing every appearance of a determination to enter and attack the port. Lord Howe improved this interval by placing his fhips in the ftrongeft pofition the channel within the Hook would admit. He
founded

founded its feveral depths in perfon; he afcertained the different fetting of the currents, and from the obfervations thus made, formed different plans with a view to the points of wind with which D'Eftaing might refolve to crofs the bar. Thefe plans, with the grounds on which they refted, he daily communicated to the commodores and captains, foliciting their opinions, and defirous of profiting by their objections. His line he lengthened by the addition of the Leviathan ftore-fhip, manned by volunteers for the occafion, and fupplied with cannon from the train. A battery of two howitzers, and one of three eighteen pounders, were erected on the point round which the enemy muft have paffed to enter the channel; while four regiments, under the command of Colonel O'Hara, were ordered by General Clinton to the Hook, left the enemy fhould attempt to poffefs it, and annoy us from fo dangerous a quarter.

In the mean time, we had the daily mortification to fee feveral of our traders fall into the enemy's hands. The Stanley armed brig, commanded by a gallant young man, fon to Sir Charles Whitworth, with five prizes, anchored in the midft of their fleet, during the night, thinking them to be Britifh, and was boarded before he could difcover the miftake. Several tenders, however, and advice-boats, efcaped

over

over the flats, and prevented the Hope, with a convoy from Halifax, from adding to our loffes and indignation.

From the time the French fquadron firft anchored off Shrewfbury, boats and fmall veffels were feen conftantly paffing to and from the fhore, for fupplies of water and provifions. On the 21ft of *July* this intercourfe was obferved to ceafe; and it was, in confequence, fuppofed that fome movement was in agitation. The fucceeding day proved our conjectures to be well-founded. The wind blew frefh at north-eaft, and by eight o'clock D'Eftaing, with all his fquadron, appeared under way. He kept working to windward, as if to gain a proper pofition for croffing the bar by the time the tide fhould ferve. The wind could not be more favourable for fuch a defign; it blew from the exact point by which he could attack us to the greateft advantage. The fpring tides were at the higheft, and raifed that afternoon thirty feet on the bar. We confequently expected the hotteft day that had ever been fought between the two nations. On our fide all was at ftake. Had the men of war been defeated, the fleet of tranfports and victuallers muft have been deftroyed, and the army, of courfe, have fallen with us; yet, under Heaven, we had not the leaft doubt of fuccefs. D'Eftaing, however, had not fpirit equal to the rifk; at three

o'clock

o'clock we saw him bear off to the southward, and in a few hours he was out of sight.

On reading this account, the public must have felt some portion, at least, of the rage and indignation that were mingled with this spirit of heroism in our brave fellows, while they reflected on their situation. They could not but consider themselves as forgotten, abandoned, marked out as sacrifices to the dastardly councils or interested designs of the first lord of the admiralty. If the sailing of La Mothe Picquet had not been a sufficient indication of the hostile designs of the French, and of their views on America, yet was it known for certain that the Toulon squadron had sailed for that country in the middle of April. The accounts were communicated to administration the latter end of that month; yet the 29th of July had not brought a single ship to reinforce our fleet, or enable us to meet the enemy. Had the French squadron arrived a few days sooner, or had the evacuation of Philadelphia been deferred a few days later (and the inauspicious appearance of the new commissioners had well nigh effected it) the whole force of Great Britain on that side the Atlantic must have been annihilated. D'Estaing would have surprised Lord Howe in the Delaware, with two ships of 64 guns, one of 50, two of 40, and a few frigates, encumbered with a fleet of transports,

C   victuallers,

victuallers, and private traders, laden, for the
moſt part, with the refugees from Philadelphia,
their families, and the wrecks of their fortunes.
All the conduct of this ſkilful commander muſt,
in that criſis, have been ineffectual ; all his cou-
rage could have done, or the bravery of his officers, would have been to ſell their lives at the
deareſt price ; and add, to the other miſeries
of their country, the loſs of ſome of the moſt
gallant men ſhe hath ever produced. General
Clinton would have reached the ſea-ſide, in the
vain expectation of meeting his tranſports. His
army fatigued ; the whole rebel force in his rear;
no proviſions, no proſpect of procuring them ;
no poſſibility of a retreat ; an enemy's ſquadron
perhaps riding in triumph, where he expected to
find a faithful aſſociate, in whoſe diſintereſted
zeal he had learned to place the moſt boundleſs
confidence. and the ſureſt hopes of a retreat, after
he had acted his own part ; ſuch would have been
the inevitable ſituation of this *ſaving phyſician* ;
he would have met, as the rebels prognoſticated
to him, the *fate* of Burgoyne, without meriting
his *diſgrace.*

At the ſame time, we heard it was boaſted at
home, that the nation had forty ſail of the line
ready to put to ſea on the moſt ſudden emergency. From the immenſe ſums that had been
granted for the navy ſupplies, and the length of
time

time adminiftration had had to guard againft the
defigns of our natural, and at all times perfidious
enemy, the boaft gained credit; but our aftonifh-
ment and indignation were only the more en-
creafed. Could the firft lord of the admiralty
talk the nation into a belief that all this force was
requifite for our home defence, while, with the
fame breath, he reprefented the French navy fo
much inferior to the Britifh? Could he make
them believe, that, from forty fail of the line, per-
fectly equipped, not the fmalleft reinforcement
could be detached, at the only time when fuch a
ftep could prove effentially ferviceable, to the relief of thirty thoufand Britifh fubjects, and a refpectable part of the navy, expofed to almoft certain ruin? Succours were indeed promifed; but
almoft three months had elapfed, and we ftill
looked for them in vain. Boiling with indignation and the thirft of revenge, in vain we caft
our eyes each hour towards the fea, in the anxi-
ous hope of feeing the Britifh colours advancing
to our relief. Little did we imagine that they
were kept idly waving in the harbour of Portfmouth, for the entertainment of *fops and holi-
day dames!*—Providence alone interfered in our
deliverance; nor can we defire a more encou-
raging proof that Heaven has not yet utterly
abandoned this nation, than thefe tranfactions ex-
hibit. The French fleet had a tedious paffage.

After

After arriving on the coaft, twenty-four hours were thrown away in chacing the Mermaid, and they afterwards remained forty-eight hours at anchor in the Delaware. Lord Howe (for this depended on his own vigilance and activity) had the earlieft intelligence of their approach; was inftantly informed of all their movements. He had time to place the fleet of tranfports in fafety ; to fee the army equally fecure ; to concentre his forces, and form fuch difpofitions, as, in the end, effectually difappointed the fanguine hopes of the rebels, and their faithlefs allies, and defeated the chief object of this boafted, and admirably concerted expedition. We experienced, no doubt, the worft of infults and mortifications. A Britifh fleet blocked up by a fquadron of Frenchmen! and in our own harbour! Veffels, bearing Englifh colours, daily captured in our fight! To have gone out to their affiftance, even had it been practicable, would have been the extreme of madnefs, fince to have been able to defend ourfelves where we lay, would, in the opinion of the moft gallant officers in the fleet, have been the utmoft that human valour could accomplifh. Yet a gentleman, who at the time obtruded himfelf into the fociety of thofe officers, who, in their company, was the loudeft in bewailing our deplorable fituation, and the defperate card Lord Howe was forced to play—whofe invectives

againft

againſt the firſt Lord of the Admiralty, as evidently defigning, by a delay of fuccours, to de-
ſtroy or difgrace the Vice Admiral, were the moſt
pointed and virulent. This gentleman now he-
ſitates not to affert, that Lord Howe enjoyed a
ſuperiority over the French Commander, and
fhould be accountable to the public for not having availed himſelf of this ſuperiority. I write
not from the information of the ſhamelefs Editor
of the Morning Poſt. That he hath hazarded
this affertion to men in power, I know from the
moſt refpectable authority. Yet this man was
once a fea officer! The lifts of both fleets lie before the public; let them anfwer this very experienced captain.

Nor can that gentleman be offended if his affertions on this fubject be efteemed, by the writer
of this narrative, fo rafh and ignorant as to deferve no other refutation than what muſt occur
to the meaneſt capacity—to thoſe who are the
leaſt converfant in navy matters. The fame lifts
fhall ſtand in oppofition even to higher authority;
to the authority of the great Lord who fo *worthily*
prefides over the navy department. For he too,
from his place in parliament, when called upon
officially to quiet the fears of the people, bluſhed
not to have recourfe to mifinformation and falfe-
hood—Dared to impofe upon the nation in a
point wherein her moſt effential and deareſt in-
tereſts

4

terefts were at ftake, and folemnly declared the Britifh Vice Admiral in America, to be at the head of a fleet equal to his defence againft all the attempts of the Toulon fquadron, independent of any fuccours from home. His heart, at the time, gave him the lie. He well knew that had the Britifh Vice Admiral in America been able, *in confequence of the advice received in May*, to collect his fleet, fcattered from Halifax to the Gulf of Florida, for the purpofe of diftreffing the rebel trade, yet he could only have had the Raifonable of 64, the Centurion of 50, and the Rainbow of 44 guns in addition to his force at New York, when D'Eftaing, *who had failed in April*, fhould firft arrive on the coaft. But perhaps I wrong the noble Lord; he no doubt meant honeftly. As a landfman he might have fuppofed, that the equality or inequality of fleets confifted only in the comparative number of fhips, however difproportioned they might be in number of guns, weight of metal, or refpective complements of men. As a landfman, his Lordfhip might not have known, that in the fummer feafon, from the prevalency of the fouth-weft winds, the voyage from Halifax to New York, is nearly as precarious as it can be from Portfmouth; or that, as Halifax is the only harbour where the large men of war could repair whatever effential damages they might have fuftained in their win-
ter

ter and fpring cruizes, it was more than probable fome of them fhould be then confined at
that port. The candid public will, no doubt,
admit this fair and fatisfactory apology. The
virtuous and untainted character his Lordfhip
enjoys in private life, muft remove every fufpi-
cion of treachery in nis official conduct. A man
fo good, a patriot fo incorruptible, could never
hazard the glory and fafety of his country, and
the blood of her citizens, from a felfifh pique;
in the narrow view of difgracing a man, whofe
fame he is faid to envy, whofe character and
principles may hold him in awe. Ignorance in
the bufinefs of his department, is his Lordfhip's
misfortune, not his fault; and it would be unfair
to affign any other caufe why he fhould retain
our fleet in port for the parade of a naval review,
at a time, when from every information the Miniftry had received, the fate of England might
have been decided in America, and thoufands of
Britifh fubjects or butchered, or reduced to thral-
dom.——But more of this hereafter.

The French fquadron continuing to ftand to
fea on the afternoon of the 22d of July, inftructions were fent to the advice boats, that were ftationed on the Flats without the Bar, to follow
and obferve their motions. From the unanimous
report of the people of the country, who efcaped
to us from the Jerfey fhore, as well as from
D'Eftaing's

D'Eftaing's movements, previous to that afternoon, it was gathered that the enemy's defign
was to force the port of New-York. It was not
unreafonable therefore to fuppofe, that their bearing away to the fouthward, was owing to the appearance of an eafterly gale, which, as it fhould
blow directly on the coaft, muft have rendered
their former fituation extremely dangerous, and
that their return might fpeedily be expected.
Advice however was received, that they were
feen on the morning of the 23d, about thirty
leagues from the land, in the latitude of the
Delaware, fteering by the wind, which was then
at eaft, on the larboard tack. The Delaware frigate was ordered on the look out, and we, at the
fame time, received an unexpected acceffion of
force by the arrival of the Renown from the Weft
Indies. [*July* 26.] Even a fingle fifty-gun fhip
was then of fuch infinite confequence to us, that
it was matter of exultation in the fleet to learn
that fhe had paffed unnoticed through the rear of
the French, in the dufk of the preceding evening.

The fame day the Difpatch returned from Halifax. As the Admiralty had given Lord Howe
to underftand, that Byron's fquadron was deftin-
ed for that port (why they fhould have been de-
ftined for that port, was not within the powers of
common fenfe to guefs) his Lordfhip had ordered

ed this floop thither on the firft certain knowledge
he had that the French fleet were advanced to
the Delaware. Her difpatches brought no mention of Byron; but they made fome amends, by
informing the Admiral, that the Raifonable and
Centurion were on their way to New York, and
in two or three days they both joined us in fafety.
The Raifonable fo narrowly efcaped the French
fleet, that fhe faw them the evening of the 27th,
fteering for Rhode Ifland. Had thofe fhips appeared a few days fooner, either they muft have
been prevented from forming a junction with our
fquadron, and forced again to fea, or we fhould
have had the mortification to fee them increafe
the triumph of our enemy.

The fame would alfo have been the fate of the
Cornwal, a 74 gun fhip of Byron's fquadron,
that croffed the Bar on the 30th. With indignation it was known by her report, that the reinforcement had not failed from Plymouth before
the ninth of June, that even then they were kept
beating through the Channel for three days in a
thick fog, without having received their final
orders, fo that had they been then feparated, not
a captain in the fquadron would have known his
deftination; that the Cornwal had parted from
them the 3d of July in a gale of wind, and that
from the miferable condition in which they had
at firft put to fea, from the ftate of their mafts

D   and

and rigging, and the difeafes amongft their crews, there was more reafon to tremble for their fafety than to look for their arrival.

The fortunate junction of fo many detached fhips, and their arriving at fo happy a moment, counterbalanced, in fome degree, this alarming intelligence. It was now known for certain that the French fleet had failed for Rhode Ifland ; and whatever little profpect of fuccefs, our force, even after the late addition, could open to us, yet the poft was of fuch importance, and the fate of fo large a portion of the Britifh army as formed the garrifon, of fuch infinite confequence to the general caufe, that it was imagined the Admiral would not lofe a moment in making fome attempt for their relief. The accounts received by his lordfhip, fubfequent to the report of the Raifonable, as appears from the public letters, favoured fuch an attempt. Thefe accounts intimated, that on the morning of the 29th, the French fleet had appeared off Newport harbour. That two of their frigates had entered the Seconnet paffage the fame day. That the next morning two line of battle fhips had run up the Naraganfet paffage, and anchored off the north end of Conanicut, and that the remainder of the fquadron were at anchor without Brenton's Ledge, about five miles from the town. In this divided fituation, fome opportunity

portunity might offer, of which advantage could be taken, for the relief of the garrison, and the preparations for sea were haftened with this view. The twenty-third regiment, under the command of Lieut. Col. Balfour, came down volunteers to serve on board the fleet, relieving the grenadiers and light infantry, whom Sir H. Clinton had withdrawn to be re-embodied. Two additional fireships, conftructed by the Vice-Admiral's orders, joined him at the fame time, and all things were in readinefs for sea by the firft of Auguft. But the fignal to weigh had fcarce been made, when the wind veered round to the fouthward, and not returning fair, fo as to correfpond with the time of high-water on the bar, till the morning of the 6th, we could not make Rhode Ifland before the evening of the 9th, when we anchored between point Judith and the light-houfe. From the report of the frigates fent on a-head, the French fleet were at anchor within the harbour. By this means the communication with Brenton's Neck was open, and the Vice-Admiral had an opportunity of receiving immediate intelligence, both from Sir R. Pigot and Captain Brifbane. They informed him that D'Eftaing, after having remained at anchor off Brenton's Ledge from the 29th of July, had, the afternoon before we arrived, entered the harbour under an eafy fail, cannonading the town and batteries as he paffed,

and

and receiving their fire without any material effect on either fide, and anchored above the town, between Goat Ifland and Conanicut. That the two line of battle fhips ftill kept their ftations in the Naraganfet and the frigates in the Seconnet. That the Wednefday before we appeared, it had been found neceffary to deftroy the Orpheus, Lark, Juno, and Cerberus frigates; that feveral merchantmen had been funk in the channel, to prevent the enemy from approaching near enough to attack the batteries to advantage, and that on D'Eftaing's entering the harbour, the Flora and Falcon had alfo been funk; that the men belonging to the feveral fhips were all on fhore, and encamped by themfelves, to be difpofed of at the General's pleafure.

From Sir R. Pigot he learned that the rebel army, with which the Toulon fquadron was to co-operate, was affembled on the Connecticut fhore, all round the ifland. Small parties of them had taken poffeffion of Conanicut, from whence he had previoufly withdrawn his troops, as he had alfo from all the out-pofts on the northern extremity of Rhode Ifland. Craft of all kinds were ready to tranfport the enemy to whatever part they fhould mark out for the defcent. Sir Robert had caufed feveral additional works to be thrown up on the heights adjacent to Newport, to which he meant to confine his defence,

and

and was himfelf pofted, with his chief ftrength, on Tommeney Hill, a very high eminence, that commands the principal approaches to the town.

Various were the conjectures throughout the fleet, with regard to the probable refolutions which the Vice Admiral might form in confe-quence of thofe advices. The French, with all their former fuperiority of force, now enjoyed a pofition infinitely ftronger than that on which we depended at Sandy Hook. The rebels were pof-feffed of the left-hand fhore, the whole length of the harbour. They confequently could not only annoy us on our entrance and approach from the craggy heights of Conanicut, clofe to which we muft have paft, but in the courfe of an attack againft D'Eftaing, as he then lay, bring what-ever number of guns they chofe to bear upon us from the northern extremity of that ifland. The moft fkilful officers were therefore of opinion, that the Vice Admiral could not rifque an attack; and it appears by his lordfhip's public letter, that this was alfo his own opinion : " under fuch cir-cumftances he judged it was impracticable to af-ford the General any effential relief."

The next morning totally altered the fcene. The wind had changed to the north-eaft, and blew directly out of the harbour. About eight o'clock a heavy cannonade was heard towards

the

the town, and in a fhort time the French fquadron appeared ftanding out to fea with all their fail a-board. Ten fail formed a line of battle a-head, advancing through the Middle Channel, and were joined without the light-houfe by the two fhips from the Naraganfet. Lord Howe immediately made the fignal to get under way, and the Britifh fleet ftood to fea. By this movement it was evident his lordfhip had two objects in view. To get time and fpace to form his difpofition to his wifhes, and either to profit by the fea breeze, fhould it fet in, as from every appearance it was conjectured it would, or by manœuvring to gain the weather gage from the enemy. This was an object of the greateft importance. Should his lordfhip await the French Admiral, and attack him to leeward, the firefhips, in which were placed the greateft hopes of fuccefs againft a force fo fuperior, not only could not have been brought into action, but would have alfo obliged the large frigates, which had them in charge, to remain inactive. The whole of that day was therefore employed in endeavouring by feveral mafterly manœuvres to throw the enemy to lee-ward. But they appeared to be equally attentive to the fame object; and difcovered as great folici-tude to preferve their advantages as the Englifh Admiral was to wreft it from them.

Night

Night came on. The Apollo was ordered to stand between the two fleets, within view of our lights, and by private signals to intimate the enemy's situation, as long as she could keep them in sight. By these means we found ourselves at the dawn of the next day, in the same relative position, though at somewhat a greater distance, than the preceding evening. The wind still hung to the eastward, blowing fresh. The weather was extremely thick and hazy; no prospect of a change appeared. The Vice Admiral therefore ordered the frigates which had the charge of the fireships to be informed, that should the enemy continue to preserve the weather gage, he should await their approach with the squadron formed in a line of battle a-head from the wind to the starboard. At the same time the fleet beheld him, with infinite satisfaction, take a decisive step that strongly marks his character, and shews him to be above the little fears and apprehensions of those, who, to avoid the whispers of the ignorant, act against their own judgment. It has ever been acknowledged, that any station in the line is the most improper a commander in chief can choose in the time of action. As soon as the ship, in which he is embarked, engages, his abilities can be of no more consequence or service than those of any other captain in his fleet. But to break through established customs, and be the

first

firſt to try the experiment, where malice might throw a ſneer at his perſonal bravery, required a man who poſſeſſed other qualities of mind than are merely requiſite to form the ſeaman. Lord Howe was convinced of the utility of the meaſure, and this alone determined him to purſue it. In his ſituation indeed the expediency was particularly obvious. Engaged with ſuch unequal force, the chief hope of ſucceſs was placed in the ſkill and abilities of the commander in chief, in his taking advantage of every fortuitous occurrence, and drawing every ſcruple of his little force into its proper point. He therefore ſhifted his flag on board the Apollo frigate, leaving the Eagle in the centre, and moved to a convenient diſtance to take a view of the whole line. As he gained by this a nearer obſervation of the French fleet, his lordſhip, perceiving, as we ſuppoſed, that D'Eſtaing had placed his largeſt ſhips in his van, thought proper to ſtrengthen the rear of the Britiſh to receive their attack, and made a ſignal for the Cornwal to move from the centre and change ſtations with the Centurion. About four o'clock the French Admiral altered his bearing, and new formed his line to engage to leeward. Lord Howe croſſed through the interſtices of our line with the frigates and fire veſſels, and in a few minutes after made a ſignal for the ſhips to ſhorten ſail, and cloſe to the centre. In this movement he

he was obeyed to the admiration of the oldeft officer, as indeed he had been in the feveral manœuvres he had put in practice either to gain the
wind, or preparatory to the intended attack. We
now expected every inftant to hear our rear engaged with the French van ; but in a fhort time
they again altered their courfe, and bearing away
to the fouthward, were foon, from the ftate of
the weather, entirely out of fight.

The wind at this time blew fo frefh, that our
fhips were under clofe reefed topfails ; and the
fea ran fo high, that Lord Howe would not venture on board his own fhip. He therefore made
the fignal from the Apollo, that he meant to lie
to, for the night, on the ftarboard tack, to prevent
feparation. Yet fo dark and hazy was the weather, and to fuch violence did the gale increafe,
that in the morning the blue divifion was totally divided from the fleet. The centre and van,
with moft of the frigates and firefhips, ftill kept
together. At noon the fquadron was alarmed by
a fignal of diftrefs from the Apollo, and in a few
minutes after, her main-topmaft was feen to go
overboard. The fhip, in which the writer of
this narative ferved, kept fight of the flag until
eleven o'clock that night, from which time, till
the 17th, in the evening, the greater part of the
fleet were ignorant of his lordfhip's fituation, and
under the greateft anxiety for his fate. It after-

E ward

wards was known to us, that the Apollo having loft her foremaft alfo on the night of the 12th, he had been toft about till the next day, when, as the gale moderated, he was taken up by Captain Hammond, and carried on board the Phœnix, then in company with the Centurion, Ardent, Richmond, Vigilant and Roebuck. On the 15th he difcovered the French fleet partly at anchor about 25 leagues to the eaftward of Cape May, and after having viewed their pofition, and left the Centurion to direct the difperfed fhips of his own fquadron, or fuch of Vice Admiral Byron's as might arrive to follow him, he directed his courfe for the rendezvous at the Hook. Here he found the reft of the fleet, which had alfo been much difperfed. The Roebuck appeared without her mizen-topmaft. The Raifonable brought in her bowfprit, the Cornwal her mainmaft, fprung. The firefhips were fo much damaged by the wet, as to be, for fometime, totally unfit for fervice. Befides thofe damages caufed by the ftorm, the Ifis returned much fhattered and difabled, from a gallant action fhe had fuftained for an hour and an half with a French feventy-four.

The French fleet were much more feverely handled. On the evening of the 13th, towards dufk, Captain Dawfon, in the Renown of fifty guns, fell in with the Languedoc, carrying Monfieur

fieur D'Eftaing totally difmafted. He ran down clofe under her lee, and being there haled, and ordered to fhew his colours, gave her all his upper-deck guns. He then ftood off to windward, and opening his lower ports, wore round under her ftern, and at half a cable's length, poured in three broadfides. Among other damages, he fhot away her rudder. It then was fo dark, and blew fo frefh, that Dawfon refolved to lie to for the night, in the refolution of renewing his attack the next morning. But at the firft dawn, fix French fhips hove in fight, three of which gave him chace, and three remained with the wreck.

The fame evening, and about the fame hour, Commodore Hotham, in the Prefton of 50 guns, alfo croffed the Tonnant, their 80 gun fhip, with only her mainmaft ftanding. He engaged her with the greateft advantage till night forced him to draw off, in the fame defign that Dawfon had formed, and with the fame certainty of fuccefs. But he was difappointed by a fimilar unfortunate intervention of part of the French fquadron.

A third action, as brilliant as any on record in the hiftory of the Englifh navy, was fought the fame day between the Ifis of 50 guns, commanded by Captain John Raynor, and the Cæfar of 74, with a flag at her mizen-maft, in com-

plete

plete order. Raynor, returning to the rendezvous, firſt diſcovered her force about three in the
afternoon, and endeavoured to eſcape her; but
ſhe proved the faſteſt ſailor. In a ſhort time
they were cloſe on board each other, and engaged
for an hour and half within piſtol ſhot. The
ſkill and addreſs of the Britiſh Captain, his intre-
-pidity and reſolution during ſo unequal a conteſt,
ſeconded by the ardour and bravery of his men
and officers, who all placed the utmoſt confidence
in his abilities, at length forced the Frenchman
to put before the wind, and fly with all her ſails.
The Iſis was incapable of purſuing him, having
ſuffered greatly in her maſts and rigging, at
which the enemy pointed all his guns. Raynor
directed his to better purpoſe. Bougainville loſt
his arm, the firſt lieutenant his leg, and they acknowledged ſeventy men killed and wounded.*
The modeſty and reſerve that ſtrike us in Raynor's public account of this glorious action, add
new luſtre to his gallantry; recommend him the
more forcibly to the public, and are characteriſtic
of the true hero. The Duke of Ancaſter, tho'
arrived from England only the day before we
ſailed, obtained leave to ſerve on board the Iſis,
and was greatly diſtinguiſhed during the action.

* In the Iſis 14 were wounded, and one man of the 23d
killed in the tops.

On

On the fleet being re-affembled, the attention of the Vice Admiral was inftantly directed to the fpeedy repair of the difabled fhips. The Ifis, with the Apollo and firefhips, were fent up to New York, and fuch flores ordered down as were requifite for the fupply of the fhips that could be repaired at the Hook. The Experiment was difpatched [*Auguft* 18.] to explore the ftate of affairs at Newport, and the condition of the garrifon, and the Ariel and Galatea fent to cruize, the one to the fouthward; the other to the northward. The fame day the Monmouth, one of Byron's ill-fated fquadron, with her mainmaft fprung, and her men wafted with difeafe, joined the fleet.

The effential repairs requifite for fo many fhips, unavoidably employed feveral days, during which the Vice Admiral received information that the French fquadron had returned to Rhode Ifland. The Experiment [23d] had been chafed into the Sound by three of their large fhips, and had returned to New York through Hellgate; the firft two-decker that had ever attempted that dangerous paffage. The Venus and Galatea confirmed the accounts. The latter had feen eleven fail of the line, including the two difmafted fhips, at anchor off the harbour of Newport, on the evening of the 20th, and left them in the fame fituation the following day.

J

The

The morning after Lord Howe had received this intelligence, and while he was waiting for the tide to begin croffing the Bar, the difabled fhips, except the Ifis and the Apollo, being then nearly compleated, Lieutenant Stanhope arrived from Rhode Ifland, from whence he made his efcape in a whale-boat, the Friday before, at the utmoft rifque of his life.* His information was, that he had left the French fleet at anchor off the harbour's mouth; that, as the wind had fince then continued at eaft, it was not probable they could be got in; that the rebels, in number more than twenty thoufand, were advanced within fifteen hundred yards of our works; that Sir R. Pigot was under no apprehenfions from any of their attempts in front; but that fhould the French fleet come in, he ordered him to fay, it would make an alarming change. Troops might be landed at Brenton's Neck, according to the original plan agreed upon between the rebels and the French, and advance upon his rear, and in that cafe he could not anfwer for the confe-quences.

On this information Lord Howe immediately croffed the Bar, and being joined in the night by

* He had paffed unperceived through the body of the French fleet, and coafting along the outward fhore of Long Ifland met with fo heavy a fea, as expofed his boat to be fwamped at each inftant.

the

the Experiment and firefhips from New York, and a number of volunteers for the Monmouth, failed the next morning for Newport. A reinforcement from Clinton's army was at the fame time to be fent through the Sound for the relief of the garrifon. Lord Howe was to favour their approach by drawing off the French fleet, and endeavouring to bring them to action; but being met at fea by the Galatea with difpatches from General Pigot, by which it appeared that D'Eftaing had, on the night, between the Friday and Saturday, failed from his anchorage off point Judith, and fteered in a courfe for Bofton, he detached the Nautilus, Sphynx and Vigilant to Rhode Ifland, and ftood on with his fquadron in queft of the enemy. As it was not probable that they would attempt to navigate their large fhips in their difabled ftate through the South Channel, within George's Bank, the Vice Admiral was in hopes, that by following that courfe, he might intercept them in their approach to Bofton Bay. Thefe hopes were confirmed by the Captain of the privateer-brig Refiftance, taken by our fleet on the 28th. He had been fent from Bofton the preceding Monday, to look out for the French fquadron, and pilot them into Bofton. But as he had failed down the channel, and feen nothing of them, he fuppofed they had fteered round the Bank.

The

The morning of the 30th brought us into Bofton Bay. The fleet continued under fail, while the Roebuck and Experiment were fent forward to look into the harbour, and by private fignals to intimate to the Admiral, whether the French fquadron were arrived or not ; or if arrived, where anchored. Between four and five we had the mortification to learn, by a fignal from the Experiment, that they were lying in Nantafket Road.

The next day the Vice Admiral, meaning to take advantage of a leading wind to view their pofition, was prevented by the St. Alban's running on fhore near the point of Cape Cod. He effected his purpofe, however, on the 1ft of September, when finding them fo ftrongly pofted, under cover of the ftrong works confructed on the iflands which command the Nantafket Road and Channel, that no attempt could be made upon them with the leaft profpect of fuccefs, he loft not a moment in returning to the affiftance of Newport. But he had already effectually relieved that important garrifon ; Sullivan, on the retreat of his allies, and the account of the Britifh fleet being failed in purfuit of them, thought proper to retire from before the place, charging his ill fuccefs to the failure of promife on the part of D'Eftaing.

Thus,

Thus, by a happy mixture of prudent and bold meafures, by a feries of manœuvres, which the naval tactick was fcarcely thought capable of exhibiting ; by an indefatigable zeal, and an ardent attention to take advantage of every occurrence ; by the unconquerable and perfevering fpirit with which his example infpired every officer and feaman under his command, Lord Howe, having, with forces fo unequal, defeated all the great defigns of the enemy, protected the army and the fleet of tranfports at New-York, raifed the fiege at Rhode-Ifland, and driven the French fquadron into the port of Bofton, whence their fhattered condition would not fuffer them to venture for a length of time, returned to New-York, and to the infinite regret both of navy and army, refigned the command into the hands of Rear Admiral Gambier.*

From

* The fending out fuch a fucceffor to Lord Howe, at fo critical a juncture, was the bittereft of the many infults paffed by the firft Lord of the Admiralty on the navy officers ferving in America. Gambier fucceeding to a command which required the abilities of a Howe, and being placed at the head of the gallant men who were formed under that great commander, was as degrading to them, as it might have been fatal to the nation. Let it not be anfwered, as I remember the great Lord once urged in his own defence, on an occafion fomewhat fimilar, that it was never defigned he fhould ferve as commander in chief, and that Byron was on

F   the

From this impartial detail of facts, the public shall judge between the infamous hints and afperfions thrown out by the abetors of a Sandwich and the conduct of Lord Howe. They will judge how much the nation is indebted to that good man and brave officer, whofe character they have heard fo infidoufly undermined. They will blufh at the cruel and unjuft treatment with which his fervices are repaid, and will turn their indignation againft the tools of a vicious man, who by ignorance and treachery, had well nigh facrificed—I will not fay the Britifh empire in America—that phantom is vanifhed—but the lives of thirty thoufand brave fellows who had fo long fought and bled for their country.

These brave fellows have indeed themfelves borne ample teftimony to the Character of Lord Howe. However unjuft the clafh of interefts or views of ambition have rendered fome individuals in the army in other inftances, in fpeaking of this brother they have but one voice; and from the general to the common men, all hung down their dejected heads, when they faw the preferver of the Britifh name in America fail from the coaft. No fhamelefs hireling could there mifreprefent facts

the coaft. I fpeak of a meafure adopted previous to the fortuitous departure of Mr. Byron for America, and the man had too much vanity to conceal the unexpected honour that was intended him from his firft arrival.

of

of which they had themfelves been witneffes, nor glofs over, by falfe and delufive accounts, the neglect or treachery, no matter to them whether treachery or neglect, of the timid and dilatory meafures purfued in the management of the navy at home, from the fatal effects of which his Lordfhip effectually refcued them, They owned themfelves indebted to him for their fafety and prefervation, and with the fame breath paid him their juft tribute of praife for the fignal triumph they faw him obtain over the enemies of their country. I repeat the words—the fignal triumph they faw him obtain over the enemies of their country. If the plain narrative I have given to my readers, has not warranted me in their opinion to ufe fuch expreffions, I am confident that a few reflections will make the public adopt the fame language.

For this purpofe it will be requifite to obferve to them, that Congrefs were much better informed of the real ftate of our navy in America, at the beginning of this year, than the Lord at the head of the Admiralty acknowledged himfelf to have been. Its numbers and fituation they reprefented to their new allies much more accurately than it fuited his lordfhip's views and purpofes to own to the Englifh nation. They knew that the chief object of our armaments in the American feas, was the interruption of their

trade,

trade, and the deſtruction of the ſmall veſſels they had been able to fit out. That for this ſervice five ſail of ſixty-four gun ſhips, five fifties, with a certain number of frigates and ſloops, were deemed amply ſufficient, and were alone employed. That even this ſmall force was conſtantly diſperſed along the whole extent of the coaſt, as it muſt have been to anſwer its intent. That therefore an armament in force, planned with ſecreſy, and conducted with vigour and expedition, might warrant hopes of the moſt brilliant and deciſive ſucceſs. They might attack the Britiſh ſhips in detail, and defeat them piece-meal. The men of war being once deſtroyed, the tranſports and victuallers muſt fall of courſe. Cut off from every ſupply of proviſion, every means of retreat, the whole Britiſh army muſt fall an eaſy prey. The conteſt muſt be decided by a ſingle blow, before the deſign could be ſuſpected at home, or at leaſt before any ſuccours could be ſent out to prevent the execution. Such were the juſt and well-grounded repreſentations urged by the American agents to the French miniſtry; and D'Eſtaing's expedition was planned in conſequence. A force, equal to the deſign, was in immediate readineſs. Such ſecreſy was obſerved, with regard to its deſtination, that the fleet had reached the longitude of the weſtern iſlands, before the
                                                            French

French Admiral, by a formal declaration of war, on board the feveral fhips of his fquadron, opened the fecret to his officers, and animated his men, by the profpect of the certain and eafy conqueft he fet before them.

While our enemies were thus employed in vigoroufly pufhing forward to the execution of the fchemes they had fo wifely planned for our deftruction, the firft Lord of the Admiralty thought his bufinefs done, if he could fuccced in deceiving the nation. The friends of the conftitution, and they who had the glory of their country at heart, were the only enemies he feemed to dread. Provided he could repel their attacks on his difgraceful adminiftration, he was willing to truft the national fafety and honour to chance. Hackneyed in the arts of deceit and mifprefentation, and encouraged by the flavifh obfequioufnefs of a large majority of the conftitutional guardians of our liberty, he made the groffeft appeal to the credulity of the people, whofe indignation he yet dreaded. With this view they were daily amufed with pompous accounts of the flourifhing ftate of our naval armaments; of the number of fhips, ready manned and fitted, that *could be fent out* when occafion required. The preparations of the French were reprefented as trifling and infignificant, and affurances given that on our fide the utmoft care was

taken

taken to rife occafionally beyond them, and
ftill to maintain our ufual fuperiority. Majefty
itfelf was brought forward to favour the deceit,
after having been firft deceived, and every me-
retricious artifice of pomp and fhew put in
practice to cover our weaknefs. Under the
hands of our ftate quacks, the nation affumed the
falfe and tranfient flufh of a confumptive patient,
while fhe languifhed interiorly, and her whole
frame was menaced with fpeedy diffolution. In
vain did her friends reprefent her real fituation,
folicit, threaten, attempt every expedient to ref-
cue her from the unfkilful hands that had firft
deftroyed her conftitution, and would now flatter
her to her ruin. In vain Lord Chatham uttered
his infpiration in the houfe of peers, and with that
voice which had fo often fpoke fafety and confidence to the nation, call upon the fervants of
the King, to embrace the vigorous, preventive
meafures, which under his own aufpicious adminiftration, had crowned our arms with glory and
conqueft. The hardeft bodies fparkle by collifion;
but in the cold hearts of our daftardly Minifters,
not a fpark could this great man kindle of the di-
ine flame that confumed himfelf. The effects
of his difappointment are too deeply engraved
in the heart of every true Englifhman to be forgotten. He found he had furvived the Britifh
fpirit, and gladly funk under this laft and glorious

I   exertion

exertion of his powers to revive it. Death, happily for himfelf, however fatally to his country, refcued him from the mifery and difgrace, of which his laft breath, like that of dying good men of old, was, I fear, prohetic.

Peace to his afhes! The mention of his name has deluded me from my fubject. I meant to obferve, that the moft accurate and authentic accounts daily received of the forward preparations in the French ports; the failing of the fquadron under La Mothe Piquet, and the object of its equipment, known beyond a doubt; the declaration of war, for as fuch every man of common fenfe confidered, from the firft, the refcript delivered with fuch infolence by the French Ambaffador in the name of his mafter; the exultation and triumph of the American agents, who, notwithftanding their native fagacity and cunning, could not conceal their joy at the full fuccefs of their negociations with the cabinet of Verfailles; the arrival of one of thefe agents at Toulon, and the preparations made for his reception, and the reception of Mr. Girard, on board the Languedoc, the ftale fubject of every public converfation; the large quantities of merchandize for the American markets, with which our Minifters were well informed the fleet at Toulon was loaded; the fulnefs of all thefe concurring circumftances, fo

clearly

clearly expreffive of the defigns of the French, was flighted and difregarded. At leaft what precautions were taken in confequence, but fuch as are to be found in the fine plaufible fpeeches of the Miniftry in both houfes, or as were confined to the idle, ineffectual vifits of the firft Lord of the Admiralty, to the feveral dockyards? Was not the important pafs of the Mediterranean ftill left open and defencelefs? Was a fingle fhip fent to reinforce our commander there, or to put him in a condition even to obferve the enemy, and inform Miniftry of their motions? Were not the firft accounts of the departure of the Toulon fquadron, and the courfe they held, communicated to one of our refidents by a foreign power, and by him tranfmitted home by land?

In the latter end of April, when this important intelligence was authenticated beyond a doubt, what part did our great and decifive Minifters take? They fought their battles with oppofition, but fuffered the enemy to proceed in triumph. The firft was their great object. To fucceed in it, they did not blufh to magnify to their Sovereign and to the people, the preparations, which the day before, they affected to defpife. The French fleet at Breft, was then declared to be in fuch force, that not a fhip could
be

be spared from our home defence.* The destination of the Toulon squadron was not cer-
tainly known—their sailing in the direction they
held might be a feint—if a squadron should be
detached from our fleet in pursuit of them, they
might perhaps, return to form a junction with
D'Orviliers, and give a decisive superiority over
Admiral Keppel—though seen at a short distance
from the western islands, yet they might have
proceeded so far only to cover their design the
more effectually—like Bayes's army, they might
remain concealed, hanging in the clouds, we may
suppose, till the intelligence of such a detachment having failed from our fleet should reach
them—they might then have tacked about, and,
joined with the armament at Brest, pour such
a resistless force on our coast, as must have
swept all before it.

To what an abject state must the nation be
reduced! How must her ancient spirit be broken, when a set of Ministers dare account for
their tame and dastardly conduct by such a tissue
of absurdities, who do not even scruple to pro-
fess, that they hold the understanding of our
representatives in such utter contempt, as to
think no reasons so flimsy or puerile, no measures of such desperate tendency, but they can

* See Lord North's speech.

G

be

be certain of a majority of voices to fupport them in both Houfes ; who have not even the decency to refpect the fufferings they have entailed upon us, but openly and vauntingly exult in the triumph they have gained over the wifdom and common-fenfe of the nation! The very reafons that fhould for ever exclude them from all confidence and truft, they fhamefully urge as a certain plea to gain additional credit from the people. "We were totally ignorant " of the ftate of our enemy, of their views " or defigns, and were confequently fearful of " taking a decifive ftep in one quarter, left the " attack fhould be meant againft us in another." ——— Befides the impudence and effrontery of fuch a confeffion, are they not aware that this queftion ftill occurs———Why had ye not placed the navy of Great-Britain in a ftate to defy all the attempts of her enemies, in every quarter of the globe, as before the days of your inaufpicious adminiftration it had ever been? Why was the fate of this once glorious empire made the fport of contingencies, and abandoned to probabilites and fenfelefs conjecture? Had ye not time enough to prepare for the trial? or were ye fearful that the nation would have refufed you the neceffary fupplies to defeat the intentions of her natural enemies, of which you had fuch long and manifeft warning? Did fhe

not

not comply with every demand however enormous or extravagant? Did not the public treasures flow in as copious streams as ye chose to mark out, and in the channels you directed? Were you not convinced that the purse of every individual would be open to you, if once the national wealth should be applied to its proper use, and the navy of Britain, her only natural bulwark and defence, become an object of your attention?

The fact is, our Ministry had the earliest and fullest intelligence of the time the Toulon squadron failed, of its destination, and the inevitable danger with which our forces in America were threatened, should D'Estaing succeed. But it is equally certain that, notwithstanding the immense sums that had been voted for the navy supplies for these three years past, the fleet was then so weak, shattered and out of repair, as not to afford a detachment adequate to the emergency. Almost two months were requisite to glean the old stores, that had lain rotting for years, in the different dock-yards, to strip the ships at Portsmouth of their rigging, and *splice and knot* cordage, that had been long condemned as unserviceable, to patch up masts and yards from the wrecks and remnants of a fleet, once the terror of the world; to sweep the prisons for men, infected with diseases, and unac-

customed

cuftomed to a fea-life. When, by all thefe wretched fhifts and contrivances, a fquadron of thirteen fail had been at length, we cannot fay fitted out, but fent to fea, what were the confequences? They could not ftand againft a fummer gale—Scattered and difperfed at the mercy of the winds and waves for almoft three months, the wretched remains of Mr. Byron's fleet arrived at New-York, moftly difmafted and unrigged, and their companies fo fickly, from the gaol infections brought by them on board, that in a feventy-four gun fhip, only eighty men were capable of doing duty. The Vice Admiral himfelf, in a difabled fhip, efcaped with difficulty from the French fleet : he thought it a happinefs to gain the port of Halifax, where he found part of his fquadron in the fame wretched condition with the fhip in which he was himfelf embarked. Tho' it muft be obvious to the moft ignorant and abject retainer of the Miniftry, that no expectations could, from the firft, be formed of a fquadron thus equipped; though they have been told repeatedly, that there is not an officer, ferving in the fquadron, who will not declare, upon his honour, that had the fhips been in any tolerable condition, with refpect either to men or furniture, they would not have even felt the force of the gale, by which they were fo miferably fhattered; yet have

have the abettors of the junto, with their ufual effrontery, caught at this happy circumftance. They have expatiated on the fubject with all the triumph of integrity, and a confcioufnefs of having difcharged their duty. They cannot, they fay, contend with winds and waves—accidents may defeat the beft defigns—had this gale not feparated the fleet, it would, in the common courfe of failing, have gained the coaft of America in fufficient time to defeat all the fchemes of the Toulon fquadron. To the facts which I have already related, that evidently refute this affertion, I fhall add one obfervation — The Cornwall was not kept back by this gale; half of the way fhe made alone, unretarded by the difproportionate failing of a fquadron ; yet fhe arrived not at the Hook till the 30th, and D'Eftaing had been on the coaft from the 5th.

After all, I may be told by the minifterial runners, that I have obtruded on the public a fubject too trifling and inconfiderable to deferve their attention. The fate of our navy and army in America, which appeared of fuch confequence to thofe engaged in their defence on the fpot, was far from being a principal object with our wife and prudent rulers. Their chief attention was employed in guarding the feat of the empire ; and the operations in the Channel

of

of England engroffed all their thoughts, and dried up all their refources. Here then, we may fuppofe, all is victory and triumph ! Here are no difgraces to weep over——no murmurs, difcontent, or complaint——no caufe of complaining. At home it would feem, adminiftration are under no neceffity of having recourfe to falfe reprefentations——of feeking unjuft pretexts to injure the reputation of the moft experienced and diftinguifhed officers of the navy, or to fhift the public indignation from one of their own fhamelefs junto, to a brave man, who preferved the nation from ftill greater infamy and difgrace. The juft and forgiving Sandwich difcovers no jealoufy, it would feem, of the gallant Admiral, who joined the prudence of a ftatefman to the fkill of a commander in chief, who dared to undeceive the public by his prudent conduct, and at the rifque of a temporary imputation on his own character, rather than by their deftruction; who, on difcovering how falfe and impudent the affertions of that fhamelefs Minifter had been, and the great fuperiority of the Breft fleet, returned to port, if poffible, to gain a reinforcement, rather than rifque the exiftence of the Britifh nation, in a conteft, the moft unequal and defperate.

Surely

Surely there is a point of tameneſs and paſſive forbearance, below which it is impoſſible that a nation ſhould fall! and either our miniſters have depreſſed us to that point, or the genius of Britain has deſerted her for ever, and her ancient ſpirit hath been ſo effectually broken and ſubjugated, as never to be rouſed again. Inſulted and threatened by every nation around us; engaged in open hoſtilities with France; on the eve of a war with Spain; Portugal, the child of our charity, deſerted to our enemies; Holland adding inſolence to ingratitude, and cavilling for pretexts to ſhare the ſpoils of her ancient defender and faithful ally; the empire itſelf diſmembered, and thoſe provinces from which we derived wealth and power and conſequence, torn from us for ever, and their inhabitants driven into the moſt relentleſs, inveterate enmity; the great ſources of our treaſure perhaps at this inſtant cut off, and thouſands of the people reduced to beggary, by the loſs of our Weſt-India iſlands. Such is the proſpect from abroad. At home, we are divided in our counſels: the betrayers of their country, who, in the courſe of a few years, have tumbled the nation from the height of glory, wealth, and power to which ſhe had been raiſed in the laſt reign, and overwhelmed her in diſgrace, beggary, and ruin, ſtill triumph in their deſigns; are employed,
cheriſhed,

cherished, supported in their obstinate adherence to the same measures, which experience has proved to be pregnant with ruin and destruction; while the friends of the constitution, who have uniformly opposed those fatal measures, are slighted, set aside, and branded with the opprobrious imputation of faction, and disappointed party malevolence; officers are pitted against officers in private broils, and the utmost pains taken by the Ministers to foment their jealousies, and add fuel to their animosities; some among themselves, who had once gained the esteem and confidence of their corps, whose abilities were rated high, and whose character was respected, have not been ashamed to prostitute their name to this vile business, and, for the smiles of a wicked great man, to sell themselves to endless contempt and scorn. The most gallant of our commanders, in both lines of service, who had long flourished in the opinion and favour of their king and country, we see insulted, injured, their reputation whispered away, and loaded with the disgrace and infamy which legions of angels could not have prevented from attending the ignorant, weak, indecisive plans imposed on them from the cabinet, and which their duty to their king reduced them to the necessity of attempting to execute.

I   In

In the mean time, the nation bleeds, from the fatal confequences of this mixture of folly and injuftice. While the Minifters, are diffident of thofe gallant and high-fpirited men, whom they are confcious they have bafely injured; and while they, on their fide, are incenfed at the perfidy of adminiftration, and fhocked at the profpect of ferving under a fet of men, from whofe councils nothing but difgrace and defeat can follow, our fleet remains without a commander; a ftrong fquadron of the enemy are now, and for weeks paft have been, cruizing in the Channel; and there is not a flag officer, of the leaft name, whom Lord Sandwich can afk to accept, or who, if afked, would accept, the command of an armament prepared to oppofe them.

The people vainly flattered themfelves that the meeting of parliament would have brought them fome relief and refcued the nation from this ignominious, defperate ftate. They looked up to the hereditary counfellors of the throne, and guardians of our liberty; they looked up to the country gentlemen, whofe interefts are fo deeply at ftake, and whofe independence, they hoped, was proof againft venality and corruption; they looked up to their gracious and beloved Sovereign; they were in hopes that he would have been at length undeceived; that our repeated loffes and difappointments, which muft

H   have

have wrung his paternal heart, would, at leaft, have rendered him diffident of the men from whofe counfels they had proceeded, and have made him pay fome attention to the numerous and refpectable part of both houfes of parliament, who uniformly protefted againft them, and counfelled better things. Difappointed in their hopes from a quarter whence their duty, their confidence, their affection, made them form the greateft expectations, the moderate part of the nation tremble at the probable confequences ; they fear left the patience of the people fhould be tired down, and they forced to fpeak a language that *muft be underftood.* Our hiftory affords but too many alarming inftances of the violent extremes to which the fpirit of the nation m--y be tranfported under fuch provocations.

Amidft all our afflictions, may we of the prefent age never experience that extreme of mifery! May our gracious King continue to be refpected, honoured, beloved, as his virtues deferve! May the public deteftation be directed againft the real authors of our difgrace, and confined to the only facrifices, which can be made with juftice, to an infulted, oppreffed, and indignant people.

F I N I S.

NEW PUBLICATIONS.

Printed for J. ALMON, oppofite Burlington-Houfe, Piccadilly.

AN ADDRESS to the LORDS of the ADMIRALTY, on their Conduct towards Admiral KEPPEL. 1s.

An EXAMINATION into the CONDUCT of the prefent ADMINISTRATION, from the Year 1774 to the Year 1778. And a Plan of Accommodation with America. By a Member of Parliament. Second Edition, 1s.

An authentic Copy of the Report from the SELECT COMMITTEE, to whom it was referred to confider and examine the Accounts of Extraordinary Services incurred and paid, and not provided for by Parliament, which have been laid before the Houfe of Commons in the Years 1776, 1777, and 1778. 2s. 6d.

This Report is a very proper Appendix to the Debates of laft Seffion.

REMARKS on a late ADDRESS to the Proprietors of the EAST-INDIA STOCK. 1s.

CONSIDERATIONS on the important Benefits to be derived from the Eaft-India Company's building and navigating their own Ships. 1s.

An authentic ACCOUNT of the Part taken by the late Earl of CHATHAM, in a Tranfaction which paffed in the beginning of the Year 1778. With the Letters of Lord Mountftuart and the hon. Mr. W. Pitt. Third Edition, 1s.

An ASYLUM for FUGITIVES. Part the fecond of the fecond Volume. Containing a Variety of curious and entertaining Pieces in Profe and Verfe. 1s. 6d.

The WEST-INDIA MERCHANT; being a Series of interefting Papers, fhewing the Danger of the Weft-India Iflands from the War with North America. 3s.

LETTERS on the AMERICAN WAR. Addreffed to the right worfhipful the Mayor and Corporation, the worfhipful the Wardens and Corporation of the Trinity-Houfe, and to the worthy Burgeffes of the Town of Kingfton upon Hull. By David Hartley, Efq; Member of Parliament for the Town of Kingfton upon Hull. 3s.

A LIST of the OFFICERS of the MILITIA of ENGLAND and WALES. For the Year 1779. With Lifts of the Lords Lieutenants and Agents; the Place where each Corps is now quartered; the Number of Men raifed by each County; Tables of their Pay and Arrears, and a complete Index of the Officers Names. Sixth Edition, corrected, 1s. 6d.

PROCEEDINGS of a COURT MARTIAL held at Cambridge, by Order of Major-General Heath, commanding the American Troops for the Northern Diftrict, for the Trial of Colonel David Henley, accufed by General Burgoyne of Ill-treatment of the Britifh Soldiers. 1s.

The SUBSTANCE of General BURGOYNE's SPEECHES on the 26th and the 28th of May, 1778. With General Wafhington's Letter to General Burgoyne. Fourth Edit. 1s.

A COMPANION to the ROYAL KALENDAR, for the Year 1779; being a Lift of all the Changes in Adminiftration, from the Acceffion of the prefent King, in October, 1760, to the prefent Time. To which is prefixed, a Lift of the late and prefent Houfe of Commons, fhewing the Changes made in the Members of Parliament from 1768 to the prefent Time; with the Names of the Candidates where the Elections were contefted, the Numbers polled, and the Decifions fince made by the Select Committees. Alfo the Dates when each City and Borough firft fent Reprefentatives to Parliament, the Right of Election in each Place, and the fuppofed Number of Voters. With a complete Index of all the Names. 1s. The great Sale of this Companion, during the few Years it has been publifhed, is the beft Proof of its Utility, and of the public Approbation. Being printed in the fame Size and Manner as the Royal Kalendar, it may be had bound with the new Edition of that Book.

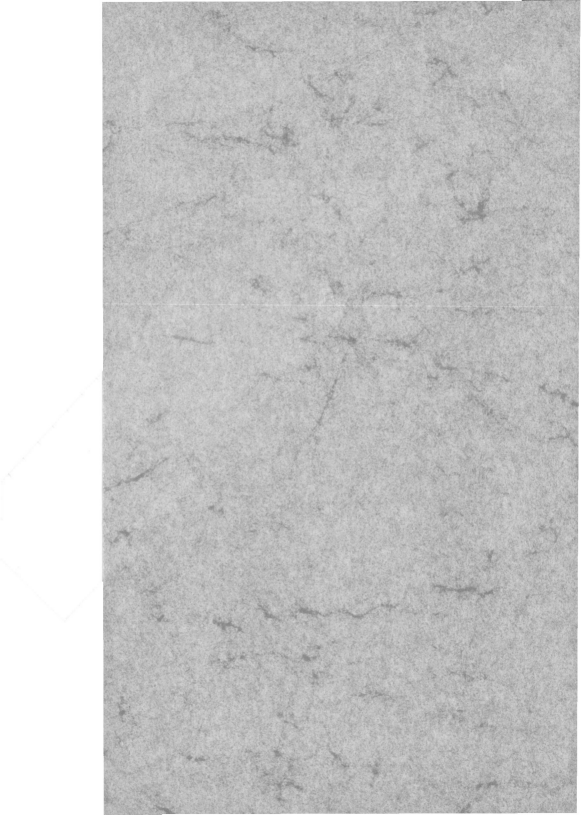

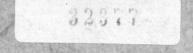
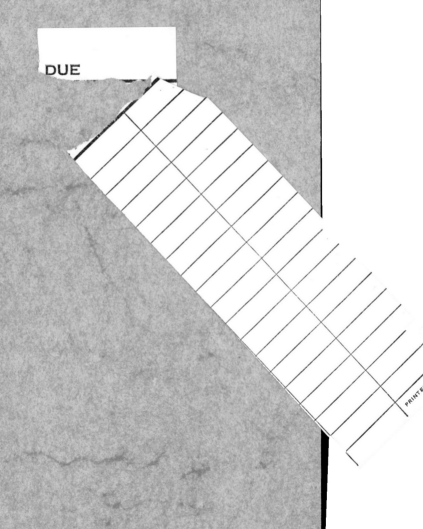